Aftermath

Tristabelle Aldrich

BookLeaf Publishing

India | USA | UK

Presentation by *BookLeaf Publishing*

Web: www.bookleafpub.com

E-mail: info@bookleafpub.com

ISBN: 9789357447706

First edition 2022

DEDICATION

This book is dedicated to my dad, whose life and sudden passing ruptured so many lives. I miss and love you, Dad.

ACKNOWLEDGEMENT

I want to say thank you to my parents for always supporting and encouraging my pursuit of writing. I also want to thank my high school creative writing teacher, Mr. Kiefer, who continued to read my work and encourage me even after I graduated.

PREFACE

This book doesn't claim to be a collection of great literary works. It's raw, written in the stages of grief, and recalls the life of a loved one from the perspective of someone they left behind. There is no organization or order, as one's emotions cannot be so easily sorted. Expectations cannot be set based on this preface, however. No one really knows what to expect from loss.

Memory

When memory is corrupted with loss,
When love is but a life not had,
When certain names I come across
I think of all the overwhelming bad.

Has there never been a time,
Where good was so much more?
Has there ever been a chime,
When we didn't look fearful at the door?

There must have been a day,
Almost like it was a dream…
That children could laugh and play,
And parents wouldn't listen for a scream.

If such a day exists I know it not.
So with my pain I live, and wish that I forgot.

Like a Switch

Some days its hard to remember.
And sometimes I forget that you're gone.
The pain never comes up slowly...
Its a switch being flipped off and on.

A picture that makes you smile one day,
Can cripple you completely the next.
A song you love and often replay,
Is laced with new context.

It's hard to find warmth in the sun,
When you can't find strength to step outside.
But without that spark in you, that passion and
fun...
What's the point of continuing life's ride?

We continue on for the days that they never had.
I wish I could be selfish. But I will live for you
Dad.

It's Not the Joke

Make me laugh.
Try "Koala" not "Giraffe".
Can you add a funny voice?
No that's not it but nice choice.

Make me grin.
"Meow" will win.
I can't say why,
But I'll laugh til I cry.

Make me weep.
It's not a leap.
Just tell it wrong...
Waterworks before long.

Make me shut down.
I see you frown.
My spark is dim.
You just aren't him.

Happy Moment

A happy moment in my life...
How could I pick just one?
Whenever my family is together,
It's always so much fun.
The best part is we never change,
And we all refuse to grow up.
Yes we're all a little strange,
But I'm proud of this family I love.

Sometimes I do wish
My brothers would calm down.
Or that my sisters wouldn't quickly switch
Who they're mad at now.

But now, as I look back,
I was always happy then.
The more memories I unpack,
The more I cherish them.

You Don't Know

You can't miss a voice you hear daily.
Not until it no longer greets you.
You don't fear a phone call from family.
Which is why a sentence can destroy you.
You can't feel the weight of your heart.
Until its ripped out of your chest.
You don't think about how you are breathing.
Except when a machine is making him breathe.
You can't know what hell is like.
Until your angel dies.
You don't know the reason for death.
And you realize Death has no reason.

Boxes

Another day gone,
Another box packed.
I'm not sure if they've moved on
Or accepted the deck is stacked.

Acceptance in defeat is hard to see
Every move will harden you more.
By the end you're cold-hearted as can be
Or shattered, spread across the floor.

But still we must keep cleaning.
Its the logical thing to do.
So I'll try not to find meaning
In a blanket or a shoe.

I won't look for you as I walk down the stairs.
Crying as boxes replace the table and chairs.

Did you?

Did you know that I was there?
Did you know I tried?
Head in hands, a hospital chair.
But not before you died.

Clinging to your hand
I sobbed and begged you
"Just get up, stand.
If you leave I won't know what to do."

How about you, did you hear?
Could you hear me plead?
Did you feel me shake in fear,
Because you know it's you I need.

A Brief Summary

A vault of trivia about anything.
The world's first talking calculator.
A calendar girl who loved to sing.
Our official snow day reporter.
Who's on first? You'd love to know.
Your favorite season? Rabbit.
A 3 hour tour?...sure. Make it so.
Find the other stooges while you're at it.

Gone

What do you think would happen,
If your mind's calming voice,
Gave your temper a choice,
And allowed that anger to step in?

How would you climb back out
Of that hole that you're digging?
Would you end up admitting
Anger heightened your self-doubt?

Or do you already know?
Are you burning bridges with purpose?
Because solitude is easier than a circus,
And a murder scarier than a crow.

But maybe you're silently screaming.
Maybe that voice just up and left.
Now you're a victim of sanity theft
And it's restoration is just you daydreaming.

Just Something

I miss your voice dad.
Not your impressions. Your voice.
I want to hear it.

Read a Christmas tale.
Sing another song to mom.
Let me hear you speak.

Call and just check in.
Say a prayer one more time.
I need to hear you.

But I know you can't.
Videos will have to do.
Until I see you.

Thank You

I think I recall a show...
One of your favorite episodes.
Christmas gifts exchanged.
One priceless and well arranged,
The other, every penny counted.
Priceless gift opened, recipient doubted
If his gift would even be enough.
Times right now are really rough.
I miss the things you did.
I'm grown up.. but I'm still your kid.
What on earth could I ever do
That would be enough to thank you?

Window

Does heaven have a window?
Hey! Can you see me up there?
If there is one, let me know.
Maybe we could share.

I'd love to see your face again,
And make funny faces at you.
We'd have a contest, but you'd win.
I would probably let you, too.

Does the window open?
Do you think that I could fit?
I might visit you a time or ten...
Or keep coming til God made me quit.

Keeping Busy

Busy every second
Because if not I'll think.
Any recovery I had made
Would be gone in a blink.

If I stopped to miss you,
If I dared to let that in,
My heart would surely wither,
Or just burst out of my skin.

So I work until I can't,
And I sleep for rest only.
When you left, they did too.
I've never felt so lonely.

But I will not think of that.
I will not face that fear.
So busy I will be...
Until I'm not useful here.

Little Details

A pair off glasses.
A walking cane.
A bologna sandwich.
A computer game.

A christmas blanket
Used all year long.
A glass of sweet tea.
An old country song.

A collection of ball caps.
A book shelf overflowing.
A cold bottle of coke
Held by someone worth knowing.

Details don't do justice...
But I can't give the full view.
Without you here beside me,
Well that will have to do.

Erased

Stories were written
And now erased.
Those words are lost,
Can't be replaced.

Gone are joy and pain,
A side you will not see.
Some much emotion written there
It felt like blood inked misery.

But now it is no more,
Wiped clean from page and mind.
Is this a loss or is it better
To forget what's left behind?

Somehow

Just another day of hurt.
There's no point denying it.
But I am warmed from within
As temperatures begin to plummet.

Maybe its the children playing
And helping each other if they fall.
Could it be my little brother's name
As my phone reads "incoming call"?

Perhaps it's just the season;
It always was a favorite.
Anticipation for autumn...
Trying ever chance to savor it.

I thought that I would hate it all.
It's just not the same this year.
Beautiful days and the people I love,
Somehow I think you're still here.

Gray Area

Water so scorching
It's almost cold.
The sky bursts with color
Yet fades at the same time.
A child laughing
But cries just alike.
Fuming with anger,
Your eyes shed tears.
Isolated showers,
On and off like a switch.
Therein lies the gray area.
Where you don't know which is which.

Inner Voice

One more day.
One last look.
No more words to say
Or desire to see what they took.

I made my choice.
Took the most important things
And I hear my inner voice:
"Go see what the future brings".

How can I enjoy a future
That I was shoved into?
Why would I want that sooner..
When I know it's without you?

Feather

Do you develop trigger words?
Do you tie them to a trauma?
Because all I wrote was "feather"
And I forgot all my present drama.

I was back in my memory
Getting out the craft supplies.
When my sister calls me...
The day that daddy dies.

Spending ten hours in a car.
Knowing it was already too late.
Machines breathing for him
But I still wanted updates.

Hospital rooms and bargaining
But nothing seemed to matter.
Sitting with siblings and talking.
Stupid mindless chatter.

No food for several days.
I wouldn't let myself sleep.
When I did the nightmares started.
I'd either scream or I would weep.

That's where I am again.
I'm having trouble getting out.
All because of "feather"
And a trauma I could have done without.